COUNTING STARS

The practice of looking up, observing the stars searching search for images started thousands of years ago. Moved by imagination, ancient Greek and Roman civilizations found shapes of exotic animals, beasts, heroes, and even common objects in the sky. The twelve signs of the zodiac, for example, came from the Zodiacal Constellations. A constellation is just a group of stars that form a pattern in the night sky that only exists in one's imagination.

Those patterns represent ancient legends and myths and had very important functions in the past. Constellations were like maps in the sky, helping people to describe the location of the planets in the solar system, to plan the planting of their crops, and also to navigate. It was much easier to find directions if you had the stars as a reference, because they're fixed points in the sky.

Scorpius

Symbol of one the twelve signs of the zodiac, this large and bright constellation is in the center of the Milky Way. At the heart of Scorpius is Antares, one of the brightest stars in the night.

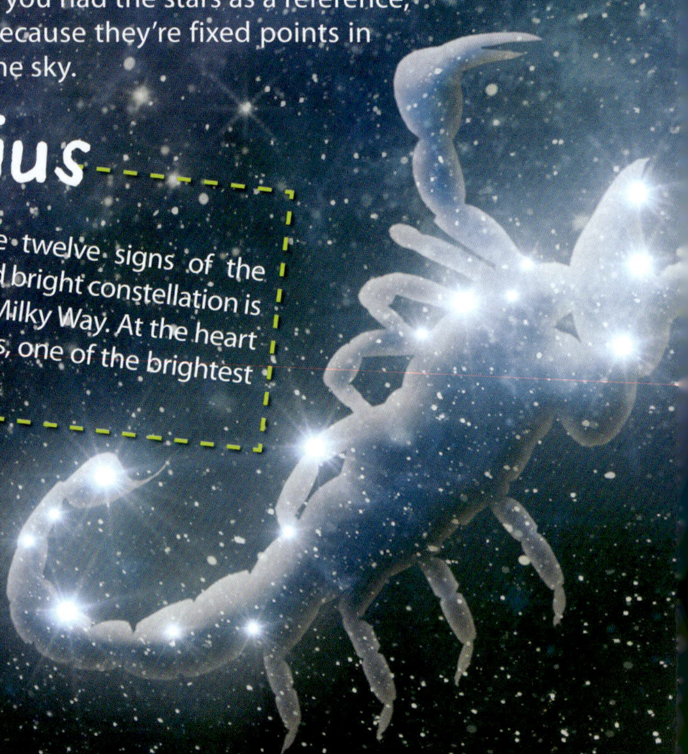

Orion

According to Greek mythology, Orion is a giant hunter. The constellation mainly consists of bright blue supergiant stars. One of them is Sirius, the brightest star in the night sky. This constellation is visible in both the Northern and Southern hemispheres.

The first picture book in history was the sky. Constellations like Aquarius, Aries, Centaurus, Orion, and Pegasus, are groups of stars that form patterns in the sky and are the objects of dreams and myths.

CURIOSITIES

- The largest constellation by area is Hydra, which is 3.16% of the sky.
- The smallest is Crux, which only takes up 0.17% of the sky.
- Most stars are between 1 billion and 10 billion years old.
- Stars don't "twinkle" as it would seem. It happens because their light travels through the Earth's atmosphere, and the turbulence affects the way we see it.

Southern Cross

The stars that form the shape of a cross are only visible in the sky of the Southern Hemisphere, where we are. Because it can be seen all year round, people use this constellation for navigation, especially to find the direction south.

Pegasus

This wonderful horse with wings is very easy to identify when you spot the Great Square. It was recognized as a constellation more than 2,000 years ago. It can be viewed from August to December.

WHAT ARE STARS?

Stars are extremely hot balls of gas. The universe is made of collections of gas, dust, and stars called galaxies. Our galaxy is the Milky Way and there are billions of stars in it. The enormous reactions taking place in stars are continually releasing energy – or electromagnetic radiation. This explains why we can see and find them through telescopes.

Five Star Street Food

Street food is a fun and delicious way to learn more about different cultures and lifestyles. It is usually more authentic and also cheaper than what you find in restaurants. However, if you want to enjoy this journey through gastronomy, it is important to forget old ideas and prejudices. It's not everywhere you can find a hot dog or some chips.

Bugs for lunch

In China, with over a billion people to feed every day, they need to be creative when eating on the street. In Beijing, you can find the world-famous noodles called chop suey but there are also some unusual dishes like bugs and insects. Silk worms, centipedes, bees, beetles, water bugs, spiders, or live scorpions may be found on sticks, fried, or mixed in soups.

According to the United Nations Food and Agriculture Organization (FAO), more than 1,900 species of insects are considered traditional foods for over 2 billion people in countries like Mexico, Ghana, Japan, and Venezuela. The organization recommends that we eat more insects and less meat. Bugs are one of the most sustainable source of nutrients and protein, so why not help the planet?

Crazy for tacos

Do you like tacos, quesadillas, and burritos? Mexico can offer you all kinds of street food made with spicy tortillas. The main ingredient of Mexican food, however, is not pepper but corn.

It was the main food for the Aztecs, who lived there when the Spanish arrived on the continent. Early Mexicans probably had been eating corn since 10,000 years before Christ. Nowadays, corn tortillas remain one of the most popular dishes eaten by Americans. This Mexican staple arrived in California in the 1960s and quickly conquered thousands of fans. In 2002, the Tortilla Industry Association estimated that Americans spent almost US$ 6 billion a year on tortillas.

Food trucks

A vehicle equipped to cook and sell food: this is the basic idea of food trucks. The truck parks in different places, and people can get food at a low cost. Nowadays, "gourmet food trucks" are also famous and may be found in dozens of countries like Australia, Canada, Argentina, and Brazil. Many chefs decided to start their careers selling creative dishes from these four-wheel restaurants. It might not be as comfortable as a real restaurant, but eating on the street is certainly an adventure you won't forget.

Fast (and great) food in Italy

During a trip to Rome, Florence, or Venice, tourists can't resist trying one of the most famous Italian creations. Pizzas are found in small shops and food markets everywhere, usually in slices. But they are definitely different from the pizza you find in Brazil. The crust in Italy is much thinner and the toppings are not as generous. The amount of cheese is minimal: a few slices of mozzarella and nothing else. Italians also don't appreciate in their pizza some ingredients Brazilians are used to, like chicken and corn. If you want to taste something different from pizza but just as delicious, try focaccia and panini.

Flavors of Mexico

DIY

This colorful country has some of the best food in the world. Cooking like a Mexican is not too difficult: try this recipe and feel like a chef!

Mexican baked potatoes **4 portions**

Instructions

1. Ask an adult to help you to preheat the oven to 200 degrees Celsius and to dice the ingredients.
2. Pierce each potato with a knife and place in the microwave for 7-9 minutes, turning every 3 minutes or so.
3. Cut potatoes in half and then cut little squares into the potato flesh.
4. Place potatoes on an oven tray lined with baking paper and spray lightly with oil.
5. Sprinkle over the potatoes half of the diced onion, the garlic and the grated cheese.
6. Place in the oven for 15-20 minutes until golden.
7. Mix corn with tomatoes, the rest of the onion, coriander, and tabasco. Season with salt and pepper.
8. Serve the tomato salsa on top of the potatoes with a dollop of sour cream or chilli beans.

Ingredients

- 4 large potatoes;
- Olive oil;
- 2 small red onions (diced);
- 1 garlic clove (diced);
- 4 tbs* of cheese (grated);
- 1 can of sweet corn;
- 2 large tomatoes (chopped);
- 1 tbs of coriander (finely chopped);
- 1 tsp* of tabasco or other hot sauce;
- 8 tsp* of light sour cream or chilli beans.

To make a light sour cream, mix a cup of yogurt with the juice of half a lemon and place it in the fridge for half an hour. You can buy the chilli beans in a supermarket.

*** tbs** = tablespoon
*** tsp** = teaspoon

You've Been Hoaxed

Strange news going viral is not new at all; it's been around for centuries and some of it has even changed history.

They say a lie told a thousand times becomes true. That's sort of what happens when a hoax is spread on the Internet. The word "hoax" means, literally, something fake, a trick. However, its online meaning has more to do with the term "rumor". A hoax is a lie, spread mostly by the media and social networks, that goes viral and ends up making a fool of lots of people.

Hoaxes can be spread as practical jokes but end up taking larger proportions. In some situations, the creator's intention is to harm a person's or corporation's reputation. These rumors can also be used as publicity, to generate buzz.

A long, long time ago

Although hoaxes are popular on the Internet, they've been around for a while. One of the most famous took place in the USA, in 1938, when writer Orson Welles read his story "Invasion of the Martians" live on CBS radio station. Uninformed people that turned on the radio in the middle of the show didn't know it was fictional and panicked.

Some of the best Internet hoaxes ever

- An e-mail chain spread the word that Bill Gates would give away money to those who forwarded it to all their contacts in 1997;
- In 2014, fake news said that Justin Bieber "saved" a Russian fisherman from a bear attack; his song "Baby" supposedly scared away the animal;
- A video posted in 2007 said you could charge your iPhone by plugging it to an onion;
- Every now and then, someone says that the cast of *Friends* is making a reunion TV show or movie; it's never true.

EMOJI the New Global Language

Do you chat with your friends online? If you look at these messages again, there's a big chance you will see more symbols and images than words. It might be a heart, a smiley face, a gesture, an animal, an object, or even a fruit.

This is how people prefer to communicate today. According to a study from Bangor University, in the United Kingdom, four in ten British people send messages made only with "emojis." Any doubt this is the new language of the 21st century?

The word emoji comes from Japanese and means "picture word." These cool symbols were created in 1999 by a Japanese engineer to facilitate communication in text messages. That's why you can see emojis like sushi, Japanese dolls, and Mount Fuji.

Today, there are 845 emoji characters supported across platforms like Android, iOS (Iphone or Ipad), Mac, and Windows.

Check out the meaning of some emojis and choose your favorite one!

MEASURING THE WORLD

What time is it? How much milk do you drink? What is the weather like? How much do you weigh? How tall is that mountain? All those questions have one thing in common. To be answered, it is necessary to use a measurement unit, like days, centimeter, kilos.

Time, volume, space, temperature, mass, and length are some things we need to measure. But don't think the measurement units are the same everywhere. If you go to any city in the USA and say you're 1.60 meters tall, people probably won't know what you're talking about. In England, for example, they might try to sell you a pint of milk.

In some manners, all countries have either legally adopted the International System of Units, or SI: the modern metric system that unifies measurement units for almost everything. Nevertheless, some cultures are so used to the old units that they have a hard time changing.

In the U.S. Customary System for example, there are more than 300 different units to measure various physical quantities. It might seems confusing, but if you have used them your whole life, would you be able to change?

Metric system to U.S. units conversion

Dimensions

Length	
Metric unit	**U.S. Unit**
1 mm	0.03937 inches
1 cm	0.3937 inches
1 m	3.281 feet 1.094 yards
1 km	0.6214 miles

Dimensions

Area	
Metric unit	**U.S. Unit**
1 mm^2	0.001550 sq. inches
1 cm^2	0.1550 sq. inches
1 m^2	10.76 sq. feet 1.196 sq. yards
1 km^2	247.1 acres miles 0.3861 sq. miles

Temperature

Celsius	Fahrenheit
-17.78	0.0
0	32
10	50
20	68
30	86
50	122
100	212

Weight

Metric unit	U.S. Unit
1 g	0.03527 ounces
1 kg	35.27 ounces 2.205 pounds
1 t	2'205 pounds 1.094 yards

The Greatest PREDATORS on Earth

Some of them may not even look scary, but they're all carnivores and very skillful hunters

Lions, eagles, tarantulas, crocodiles, and Komodo dragons: what do these animals have in common? They don't belong to the same families nor do they live in similar environments, but they share one important feature: they're all predators. It's not a matter of size or ferocity; it's all about the skills to observe, capture, and feed on other species. What some of these predators may lack in size, they make up in keen hunting abilities and lack of mercy for their prey.

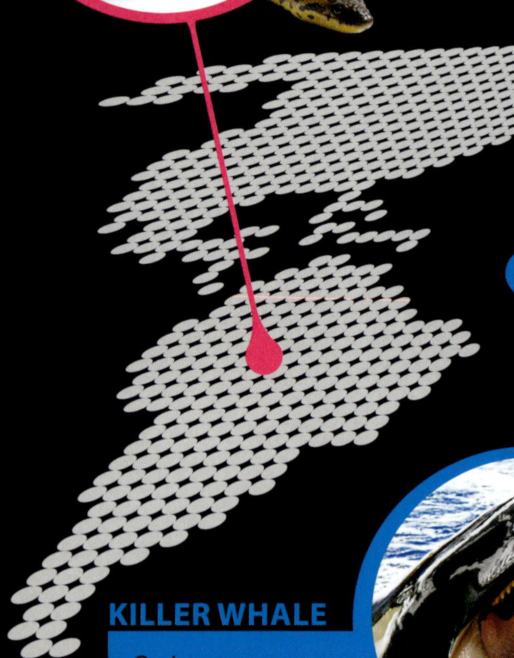

ANACONDA

Eunectes murinus

Size: up to 9 m in length

Weight: up to 300 kilos

Natural habitat: flooded areas of South America, such as the Pantanal in center-western Brazil; they spend most of their time under water, but often come to the surface to hunt.

What they eat: they prey on animals of different sizes and species – some even bigger than themselves, which can at times cause their death; they are known for devouring cattle from farms, but, when in the forest, they can eat anything from fish to mammals, like the tapir.

KILLER WHALE

Orcinus orca

Size: up to 9 m

Weight: up to 6 tons

Natural habitat: groups of killer whales (that belong to the same family as dolphins), formed by around nine animals, may be found in all oceans.

What they eat: all kinds of sea species, from birds that fly over the coasts to sharks or smaller whales.

POLAR BEAR

Ursus maritimus

Size: up to 2.5 m in length

Weight: up to 8 tons

Natural habitat: they live alone in the Polar Arctic region; these animals will only "socialize" during breeding periods.

What they eat: main courses are mostly different types of seals, but they can eat pretty much anything, like birds, fish, penguins, plants, and the carcasses of whales and walruses.

BENGAL TIGER

Panthera tigris tigres

Size: up to 3.1 m in length

Weight: up to 260 kilos

Natural habitat: they live in many different areas of India and in a few border countries.

What they eat: they hunt and devour animals of many species, such as birds, monkeys, crocodiles, pythons, and even other predator mammals, like wolves and leopards.

GREAT WHITE SHARK

Carcharodon carcharias

Size: up to 7.5 m in length

Weight: up to 2.5 tons

Natural habitat: coastal areas in the Americas, Oceania, Asia, Africa, and Europe, where water is shallow and warm, with plenty of food to hunt.

What they eat: fish and sea mammals are the most important meal in an adult's menu; sharks don't feed on people, they feast on greasy meat that can help them spend long periods of time without eating. Unfortunally, they can't know that before taking a bite.

Frozen Winter Fun

Every four years, the world celebrates peace and friendship between nations with the Olympic Games. This tradition is much older than we can imagine: it began at Ancient Greece, in 776 BC, in the city of Olympia. The games celebrated Zeus, the God of the Greeks, and also meant to show the physical qualities of young people. Running, jumping, and boxing were some of the sport events by that time.

The modern Olympics started in 1896. But they basically include summer sports, like gymnastics, swimming, and cycling. Many nations from the Northern Hemisphere – where winter is extremely cold and long – decided to create a separate competition for the winter sports: the Winter Olympics.

Snowboarding

Snowboarding is considered a very dynamic sport because it combines elements of three different activities: surfing, skateboarding, and skiing. To be a winner, riders compete for spend, height, or the style of their tricks. There are four basic events: the halfpipe, the parallel slalom, the cross event, and the slopestyle event.

This sport was developed in the United States in the 1960s, but it only became a Winter Olympic event at the Nagano Games (Japan), in 1998. More than 80 nations and 6,700 athletes compete during the Games.

Luge

The famous Santa Claus vehicle is the main equipment of this traditional sport. "Luge" is the word in French for "sled". Luges are made of fiberglass and can speed up to 90 miles per hour – or 140 Km/hour. And there are no brakes to stop the sled. That explains why it is the most dangerous sport at the Olympic Games.

Luge can be practiced by 1 or 2 racers. They use their hands to get going while sitting on the sled and then lie on their backs all the way down the track. According to the rules, there are four races over two days of competition.

The fist Winter Olympics was held in Chamonix, France, in 1924, with more than 200 athletes from 16 nations. Since then, it happens every four years, in host cities in countries like USA, Canada, Austria, Germany, and Japan.

Today, there are 15 winter events. They are usually practiced on ice, like ice hockey and figure skating, or in the snow, like ski jumping and alpine skiing.

Where DOES Rock and Roll MUSIC come from?

In the late 1940s a wide range of music was popular in America – gospel, jazz, Western swing, country, jump blues, boogie-woogie, and others – especially in the South. You listened to the music you liked on your favourite local radio show, or by buying and playing single tracks, or by hearing music live, just as we do now. No downloads though! The tracks were sold on records known as 78s.

When African-American people from the South began to move north to find work, their music travelled with them to larger cities, spreading across the whole United States.

Rock!

Who is the King

LITTLE RICHARD

Some people think an African-American singer called Little Richard is the real King of rock 'n' roll. Richard Penniman began as a gospel singer, and taught himself to play saxophone and later piano. He left home at 16 to tour with a travelling rhythm and blues show.

His first hit record, *Tutti Frutti*, was popular on rhythm and blues and on "pop" music sales charts. Between the 1955 and 1957 he had 18 hit singles.

Little Richards influence can be heard in soul, funk, and hip-hop, as well as in rock and roll. James Brown and Elvis Presley have spoken about his importance. So have Bob Dylan, Jimi Hendrix, Michael Jackson, and even Bruno Mars, among others.

Rock!

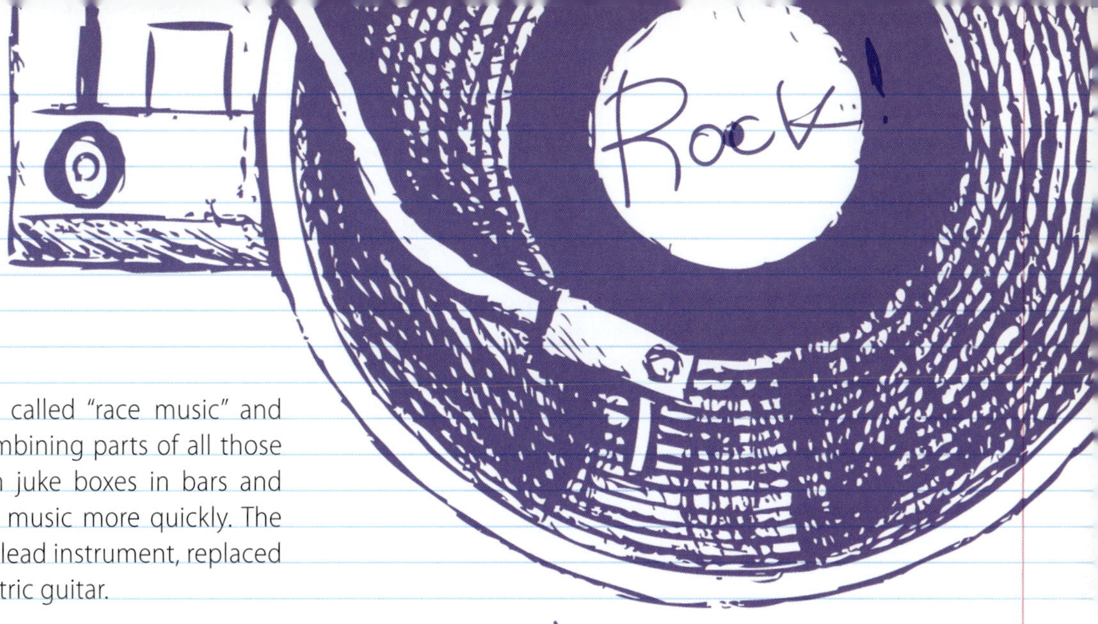

A new style emerged, first called "race music" and then "rhythm and blues," combining parts of all those rhythms. Records played on juke boxes in bars and shops helped to spread the music more quickly. The piano or saxophone was the lead instrument, replaced during the 1950s by the electric guitar.

Rock!

But the first song to be really called "rock and roll" was a gospel song called *Rock Me*, recorded by Sister Rosetta Tharpe in 1942. A review in music magazine Billboard called it "rock-and-roll spiritual singing", and it does sound much more like a rock song than an old-fashion church hymn!

# of Rock'n'Roll?

ELVIS PRESLEY

Elvis Aaron Presley is called The King. He was the first white American rock 'n' roll singer to become very popular, helped by a long series of films in which he sang and acted.

In 1954 during a recording session, Elvis picked up his guitar and improvised a blues song by Arthur "Big Boy" Crudup, called *That's All Right*. Three days later a popular Memphis radio DJ played it and had so many telephone calls from his listeners that he played it over and over again during the last two hours of the show. Elvis had begun his rise to world-wide popularity.

Quiz

WORD PUZZLE
FIND THE NAMES OF THE GALAXIES

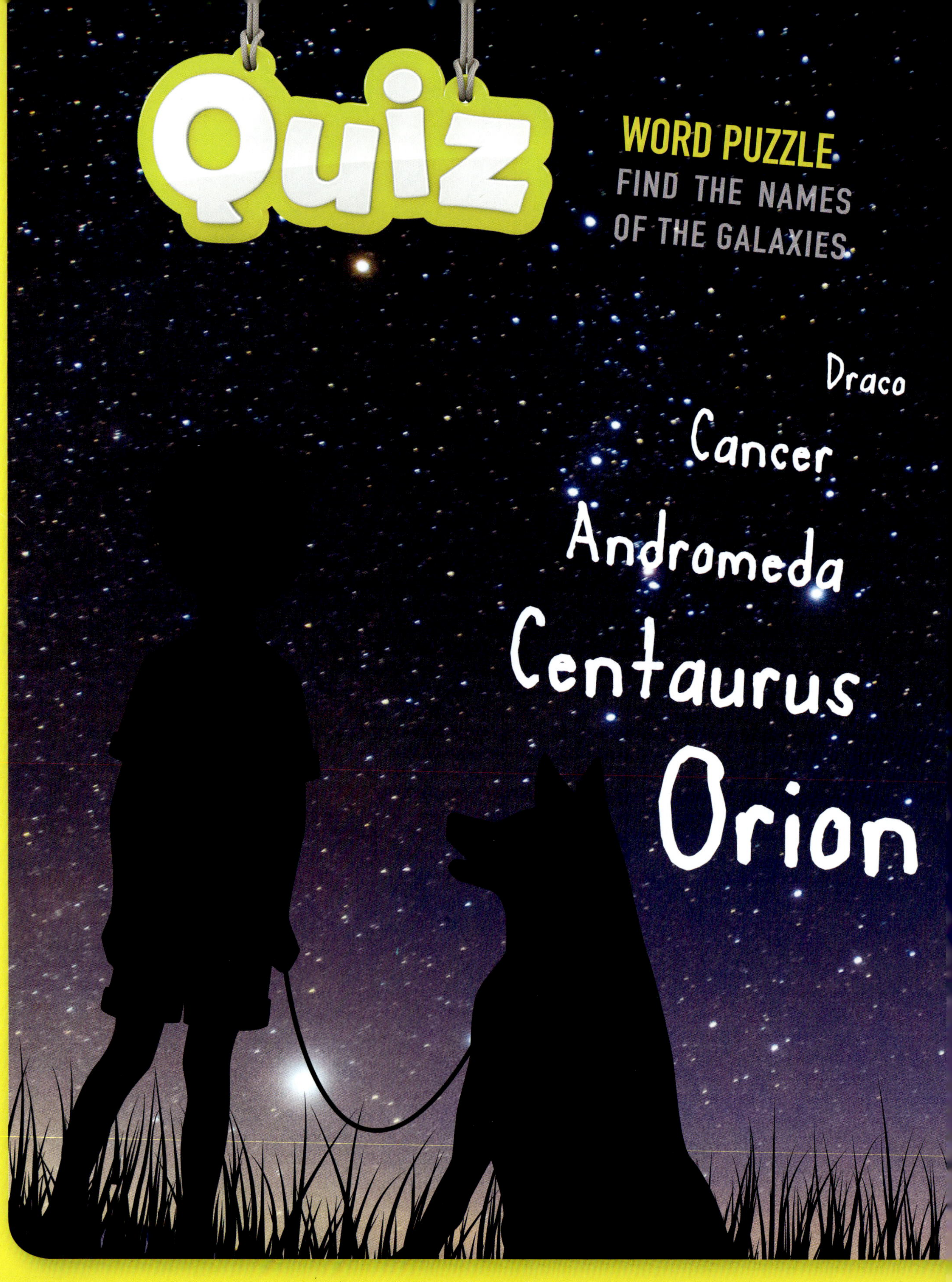

Draco
Cancer
Andromeda
Centaurus
Orion